TEACHERS ARE...

TEACHERS ARE...

Written and Edited by Jill Wolf

ISBN 0-89954-444-4
Copyright © 1992 Antioch Publishing Company
Yellow Springs, Ohio 45387

Printed in the U.S.A.

CONTENTS

Sharers of Wisdom   6

He teaches who gives and he learns who receives.
—*Ralph Waldo Emerson*

Sources of Inspiration   15

The true aim of every one who aspires to be a teacher should be...to kindle minds.
—*Frederick W. Robertson*

Examples of Excellence   32

...may their teachers be examples of excellence in scholarship and character...
—*Author Unknown*

Followers in His Footsteps   43

A large crowd came to Him, and He began to teach them.
Mark 2:13 (NIV)

Special, Valued, and Honored Friends   48

Thou wert my guide, philosopher and friend.
—*Alexander Pope*

SHARERS OF WISDOM

—Teachers are sharers of the priceless gift of wisdom, a gift more precious than any material thing.

—Teachers are sharers and partners in discovery. They help us find the facts we need to know, while helping us find out about ourselves and our abilities.

—Teachers are sharers in the process of learning, for by teaching others, they learn new things also.

—Teachers are sharers not only of information, but of ideas. They are givers not only of answers, but of ways to find answers.

—Teachers are sharers of enthusiasm, who impart to us the joy and love of learning.

—Teachers are sharers in the present and the future, for they affect not just one student, but whole generations, communities, and countries.

—Teachers are sharers of their time, energy, knowledge, and, most of all, themselves.

If you have knowledge, let others light their candles at it.

—*Thomas Fuller*

Those having torches will pass
them on to others.

—*Plato*

Our knowledge is the amassed thought and experience of innumerable minds.

—*Ralph Waldo Emerson*

The wealth of mankind is the wisdom they leave.

—*J. B. O'Reilly*

Wisdom alone is true ambition's aim,
Wisdom the source of virtue, and of fame,
Obtained with labour, for mankind employed,
And then, when most you share it, best
    enjoyed.

—William Whitehead

Choose my instruction instead of silver,
knowledge rather than choice gold, for wisdom
is more precious than rubies, and nothing you
desire can compare with her.

Proverbs 8:10,11 (NIV)

The greatest good you can do for another is not just to share your riches, but to reveal to him his own.

—Benjamin Disraeli

I want it said of me by those who knew me best, that I always...planted a flower where I thought a flower would grow.

—Abraham Lincoln

Consider that I laboured not for myself only, but for all them that seek learning.

—The Apocrypha

When I am forgotten...say, I taught thee.

—William Shakespeare

He teaches who gives and he learns who receives.

—Ralph Waldo Emerson

It is the province of knowledge to speak, and it is the privilege of wisdom to listen.

—Oliver Wendell Holmes

The one exclusive sign of a thorough
knowledge is the power of teaching.

—Aristotle

Not only is there an art in knowing a thing,
but also a certain art in teaching it.

—Cicero

The man who can make hard things easy
is the educator.

—Ralph Waldo Emerson

All practical teachers know that education is a
patient process of the mastery of details,
minute by minute, hour by hour, day by day.

—Alfred North Whitehead

There is no teaching until the pupil is brought into the same state or principle in which you are; a transfusion takes place; he is you and you are he; then is a teaching, and by no unfriendly chance or bad company can he ever quite lose the benefit.

—*Ralph Waldo Emerson*

Men learn while they teach.

—*Seneca*

The twig is so easily bended
I have banished the rule and the rod:
I have taught them the goodness of knowledge,
They have taught me the goodness of God...

—*Charles M. Dickinson*

SOURCES OF INSPIRATION

—Teachers are the sparks that fire our
imaginations and kindle our dreams.

—Teachers are the sunrise that awakens
us to new ideas.

—Teachers are the lamps that light our
way along the path of knowledge.

—Teachers are the fountains that quench
our thirst for knowledge.

—Teachers are the gardeners who plant the seeds of knowledge. They are the rain and the sunshine that help those seeds—and us—to grow.

—Teachers are the builders and sculptors who shape our minds and our characters.

—Teachers are the liberators who free us from fear and ignorance. They give us the power and wealth of knowledge so that we may become the best we can be.

To know how to suggest is the great art of teaching.

—Henri-Frédéric Amiel

The whole art of teaching is only the art of awakening the natural curiosity of young minds for the purpose of satisfying it afterwards.

—Anatole France

The best teacher is the one who suggests rather than dogmatizes, and inspires his listener with the wish to teach himself.

—Edward Bulwer-Lytton

The true aim of every one who aspires to be a teacher should be, not to impart his own opinions, but to kindle minds.

—*Frederick W. Robertson*

The object of teaching a child is to enable him to get along without his teacher.

—*Elbert Hubbard*

That's what education means—to be able to do what you've never done before.

—*Author Unknown*

TO A MUSIC TEACHER

You cannot practice for her every day;
The knowledge that you give her
   will not stream
On her young mind in one bright,
   blinding ray,
But you can plant a dream.

Ah, you can plant a dream
   in her young heart,
A dream of excellence whose
   light will gleam
Upon her pathway as the years depart;
Your words can plant a dream.

To sow a dream and see it spread
   and grow;
To light a lamp and watch its
   brightness gleam;
Here is a gift that is divine, I know—
To give a child a dream.

               —*Anne Campbell*

Education, then, briefly, is the leading of human souls to what is best, and making what is best out of them; and these two objects are always attainable together, and by the same means; the training which makes men happiest in themselves also makes them most serviceable to others. True education, then, has respect first to the ends that are proposable to the man, or attainable by him; and, secondly, to the material of which the man is made. So far as it is able it chooses the end according to the material; but it cannot always choose the end, for the position of many persons in life is fixed by necessity; still less can it choose the material; and, therefore, all it can do is to fit the one to the other as wisely as may be.

—John Ruskin

The true purpose of education is to cherish
and unfold the seed of immortality already
sown within us; to develop, to their fullest
extent, the capacities of every kind with
which the God who made us has endowed us.

—Anna Jameson

As the rough diamond from the mine,
In breakings only shews its light,
Till polishing has made it shine:
Thus learning makes the genius bright.

—Allan Ramsay

THE BUILDER

A builder builded a temple,
He wrought it with grace and skill;
Pillars and groins and arches
All fashioned to work his will.
Men said, as they saw its beauty,
"It shall never know decay;
Great is thy skill, O Builder!
Thy fame shall endure for aye."

A Teacher builded a temple
With loving and infinite care,
Planning each arch with patience,
Laying each stone with prayer.
None praised her unceasing efforts,
None knew of her wondrous plan,
For the temple the Teacher builded
Was unseen by the eyes of man.

Gone is the Builder's temple,
Crumpled into the dust;
Low lies each stately pillar,
Food for consuming rust.
But the temple the Teacher builded
Will last while the ages roll,
For that beautiful unseen temple
Was a child's immortal soul.

—Adapted from a poem by
Hattie Vose Hall

A statue lies hid in a block of marble, and the art of statuary only clears away the superfluous matter and removes the rubbish. The figure is in the stone; the sculpture only finds it. What sculpture is to a block of marble, education is to a human soul. The philosopher, the saint, or the hero, the wise, the good or the great man, very often lies hid and concealed in a plebian, which a proper education might have disinterred, and have brought to light.

—*Joseph Addison*

Wonder...is the seed of knowledge.
—Francis Bacon

From the very beginning of his education,
the child should experience the joy of
discovery.
—Alfred North Whitehead

If we succeed in giving the love of learning,
the learning itself is sure to follow.
—Sir John Lubbock

The teacher who is attempting to teach
without inspiring the pupil with a desire to
learn is hammering on cold iron.
—Horace Mann

A teacher who can arouse a feeling for one single good action, for one single good poem, accomplishes more than he who fills our memory with rows on rows of natural objects, classified with name and form.

—Johann Wolfgang von Goethe

Nothing is sweeter than to dwell in the serene temples of the wise, well fortified by learning.

—Lucretius

Finally, education alone can conduct us to that enjoyment which is, at once, best in quality and infinite in quantity.

—Horace Mann

It made me gladsome to be getting some education, it being like a big window opening.

—*Mary Webb*

Only the educated are free.

—*Epictetus*

"If you hold to My teaching...you will know the truth, and the truth will set you free."

John 8:31,32 (NIV)

Knowledge is the only fountain, both of the love and the principles of human liberty.

—*Daniel Webster*

Knowledge is the antidote to fear...

—*Ralph Waldo Emerson*

Let my teaching fall like rain and my words
descend like dew, like showers on new grass,
like abundant rain on tender plants.

Deuteronomy 32:2 (NIV)

The teaching of the wise is a fountain of life...

Proverbs 13:14 (NIV)

Knowledge, in truth, is the great sun in the
firmament. Life and power are scattered with
all its beams.

—Daniel Webster

Knowledge of itself is riches.

—*Sadi*

A learned man has always wealth within himself.

—*Phaedrus*

There is no knowledge which is not valuable.

—*Edmund Burke*

A wise man has great power, and a man of knowledge increases strength...

Proverbs 24:5 (NIV)

Knowledge is power.
—*Thomas Hobbes*

There is no knowledge that is not power.
—*Ralph Waldo Emerson*

Every addition to true knowledge is an addition to human power.

—*Horace Mann*

Instruction increases inborn worth, and right discipline strengthens the heart.

—*Horace*

For the more a man knows, the more worthy he is.

—*Robert of Gloucester*

He who binds
His soul to knowledge, steals the key
    of heaven.

—*N. P. Willis*

EXAMPLES OF EXCELLENCE

— Teachers are leaders and guides, who not only tell us the way, but show us the way.

— Teachers are role models on which we can pattern our lives. They give us standards to go by, goals to aim for, and someone whom we can look up to and imitate.

— Teachers are second parents who care for our educational needs. They "feed and clothe" our minds and look after our intellectual and moral welfare.

— Teachers are shapers of the future, for they influence the lives of children and generations to come.

Education does not mean teaching people what they do not know. It means teaching them to behave as they do not behave. It is not teaching the youth the shapes of letters and the tricks of numbers, and then leaving them to turn their arithmetic to roguery, and their literature to lust. It means, on the contrary, training them into the perfect exercise and kingly continence of their bodies and souls. It is a painful, continual and difficult work to be done by kindness, by watching, by warning, by precept, and by praise, but above all—by example.

—*John Ruskin*

A TEACHER'S PRAYER

I want to teach my students more
    than lessons in a book;
I want to teach them deeper things
    that people overlook—
The value of a rose in bloom,
    its use and beauty, too,
A sense of curiosity to discover
    what is true;
How to think and how to choose
    the right above the wrong,
How to live and learn each day
    and grow up to be strong;
To teach them always how to gain
    in wisdom and in grace,
So they will someday make the world
    a brighter, better place.
Lord, let me be a friend and guide
    to give these minds a start
Upon their way down life's long road,
    then I'll have done my part.

                        —Jill Wolf

He is wise who can instruct us and assist us
in the business of daily virtuous living.
—Thomas Carlyle

That which we are, we are all the while
teaching, not voluntarily, but involuntarily.
—Ralph Waldo Emerson

Teach us by your lives.
—Horatius Bonar

A DEDICATION

Let us now with earnest hearts and with exalted faith and hope solemnly consecrate this building to its high and holy purpose. May the youth of this community for generations to come gather in this place to receive instruction in knowledge and training in virtue. May they find here every condition necessary to a true and enlightened education. Especially, may their teachers be examples of excellence in scholarship and character, seekers after goodness and truth, lovers of children, enthusiasts and adepts in the finest of all arts, the development and inspiration of human souls. May these rooms always be pervaded with an invigorating atmosphere of mental and moral life, and may no child pass from these schools to higher grades or to the outer world without having been made more intelligent, more thoughtful, more courageous, more virtuous, and in every way more capable of wise and just, of useful and noble living. To this end, may the blessing of God be upon child and parent, upon pupil and teacher, upon principal and superintendent and upon every one whose influence will in any degree affect the work of education as it shall be conducted within these walls.

—Author Unknown

Knowledge is a treasure, but practice is the key to it.

—*Thomas Fuller*

"A student is not above his teacher, but everyone who is fully trained will be like his teacher."

Luke 6:40 (NIV)

God sends His teachers unto every age,
To every clime, and every race of men,
With revelations fitted to their growth
And shape of mind, nor gives
    the realm of truth
Into the selfish rule of one sole race.
                  —*James Russell Lowell*

A teacher affects eternity; he can never tell
where his influence stops.
                  —*Henry Brooks Adams*

They who educate children well, are more to be honoured than they who produce them; for these only gave them life, those the art of living well.

—*Aristotle*

I am indebted to my father for living, but to my teacher for living well.

—*Alexander III of Macedonia*

What greater or better gift can we offer the republic than to teach and instruct our youth?

—*Cicero*

Delightful task! to rear the tender thought,
To teach the young idea how to shoot.

—*James Thomson*

Just as the twig is bent, the tree is inclined.

—*Alexander Pope*

Children have more need of models than of critics.

—*Joseph Joubert*

In praising or loving a child, we love and praise not that which is, but that which we hope for.

—*Johann Wolfgang von Goethe*

Give a little love to a child, and you get a great deal back.

—*John Ruskin*

THE TEACHER

Lord, who am I to teach the way
To little children day by day,
So prone myself to go astray?

I teach them knowledge, but I know
How faint they flicker and how low
The candles of my knowledge glow.

I teach them power to will and do,
But only now to learn anew
My own great weakness through
    and through.

I teach them love for all mankind
And all God's creatures, but I find
My love comes lagging far behind.

Lord, if their guide I still must be,
Oh, let the little children see
The teacher leaning hard on Thee.

—*Leslie Pinckney Hill*

FOLLOWERS IN HIS FOOTSTEPS

—Teachers are the volunteers who answer God's call to spread the knowledge of His word and His world.

—Teachers are God's helpers, who carry on the good work of raising people's lives to a higher level through the improvement of their minds, skills, and characters.

—Teachers are followers in the footsteps of Jesus, the greatest teacher of all.

Every year His parents went to Jerusalem for the Feast of the Passover. When He was twelve years old, they went up to the Feast, according to the custom. After the Feast was over, while His parents were returning home, the boy Jesus stayed behind in Jerusalem, but they were unaware of it. Thinking He was in their company, they traveled on for a day. Then they began looking for Him among their relatives and friends. When they did not find Him, they went back to Jerusalem to look for Him. After three days they found Him in the temple courts, sitting among the teachers, listening to them and asking them questions.

Luke 2:41-46 (NIV)

Jesus returned to Galilee in the power of the Spirit, and news about Him spread through the whole countryside. He taught in their synagogues, and everyone praised Him.

Luke 4:14,15 (NIV)

Then He went down to Capernaum, a town in Galilee, and on the Sabbath began to teach the people. They were amazed at His teaching, because His message had authority.

Luke 4:31,32 (NIV)

Jesus went throughout Galilee, teaching in their synagogues, preaching the good news of the kingdom, and healing every disease and sickness among the people.

Matthew 4:23 (NIV)

After Jesus had finished instructing His twelve disciples, He went on from there to teach and preach in the towns of Galilee.

Matthew 11:1 (NIV)

A large crowd came to Him, and He began to teach them.

Mark 2:13 (NIV)

At dawn He appeared again in the temple courts, where all the people gathered around Him, and He sat down to teach them.

John 8:2 (NIV)

"Therefore go and make disciples of all nations...teaching them to obey everything I have commanded you."

Matthew 28:19,20 (NIV)

We have different gifts, according to the grace given us. If a man's gift is prophesying, let him use it in proportion to his faith. If it is serving, let him serve; if it is teaching, let him teach; if it is encouraging, let him encourage; if it is contributing to the needs of others, let him give generously; if it is leadership, let him govern diligently; if it is showing mercy, let him do it cheerfully.

Romans 12:6-8 (NIV)

"Therefore every teacher of the law who has been instructed about the kingdom of heaven is like the owner of a house who brings out of his storeroom new treasures as well as old."

Matthew 13:52 (NIV)

SPECIAL, VALUED, AND HONORED FRIENDS

—Teachers are special friends, for the best friend we can have is one who teaches us something.

—Teachers are valued friends who inspire us to aim high, push us to do our best, praise us when we do well, help us to understand our errors and find the right way, and encourage us to try again.

—Teachers are honored friends whom we esteem and admire, for they take on the difficult tasks and the great responsibilities, asking only our respect in return—and the reward of watching us grow, learn, and become what we can be.

Thou wert my guide, philosopher and friend.

—Alexander Pope

We do not wish for friends to feed and clothe
our bodies—neighbors are kind enough for that
—but to do the like office for our spirits.

—Henry David Thoreau

WHY GOD CREATED TEACHERS

When God created teachers,
    He gave us special friends
To help us understand His world
    and truly comprehend
The beauty and the wonder
    of everything we see,
And become a better person
    with each discovery.

When God created teachers,
    He gave us special guides
To show us ways in which to grow
    so we can all decide
How to live and how to do
    what's right instead of wrong,
To lead us so that we can lead
    and learn how to be strong.

Why God created teachers,
    in His wisdom and His grace,
Was to help us learn to make our world
    a better, wiser place.

—Jill Wolf

Who kindly sets a wanderer on his way
Does e'en as if he lit another's lamp by his:
No less shines his, when he his friend's hath lit.

—Ennius

I am not a teacher: only a fellow-traveller of
whom you asked the way. I pointed ahead—
ahead of myself as well as of you.

—George Bernard Shaw

The friend who holds up before me the mirror, conceals not my smallest faults, warns me kindly, reproves me affectionately, when I have not performed my duty, he is my friend, however little he may appear so. Again, if a man flattering praises and lauds me, overlooks my faults, and forgives them before I have repented, he is my enemy, however much he may appear my friend.

—Johann Gottfried von Herder

A true friend is somebody who can make us do what we can.

—*Ralph Waldo Emerson*

A friend is one who incessantly pays us the compliment of expecting from us all the virtues, and who can appreciate them in us.

—*Henry David Thoreau*

What office is there which involves
more responsibility, which requires more
qualifications, and which ought, therefore,
to be more honourable, than that of teaching?

—Harriet Martineau

The true knight of Learning,
   the world holds him dear—
Love bless him, Joy crown him,
   God speed his career.

—Oliver Wendell Holmes

Teachers should be held in the highest honor. They are the allies of legislators; they have agency in the prevention of crime; they aid in regulating the atmosphere, whose incessant action and pressure cause the life-blood to circulate, and to return pure and healthful to the heart of the nation.

—*Lydia Sigourney*

How great a thing is wisdom! I never come near you but I go away wiser.

—*Terence*

I am not willing that this discussion should close without mention of the value of a true teacher. Give me a log hut, with only a simple bench, Mark Hopkins on one end and I on the other, and you may have all the buildings, apparatus and libraries without him.*

—*James A. Garfield*

* *Mark Hopkins was Garfield's teacher.*